How to Earn Money on Facebook with Affiliate Marketing"

Introduction

Greetings! Welcome to our guide on how to make money on Facebook with Affiliate Marketing. In this eBook, we will delve into the world of affiliate marketing and explore how you can leverage the power of Facebook to earn a passive income. We all know that Facebook is a social media giant with millions of active users, making it an ideal platform for promoting products and services.

Affiliate marketing is a simple concept where you promote someone else's product and earn a commission for each sale made through your unique referral link. With the rise of e-commerce and online shopping, affiliate marketing has become a lucrative industry and a popular way for people to make money from home.

We will take you through the steps of setting up your affiliate marketing business on Facebook, including how to choose the right products, create engaging content, and drive traffic to your affiliate offers. We will also cover the essential tools and techniques you need to succeed, such as tracking your performance and optimizing your campaigns for maximum profitability.

By the end of this eBook, you will have a solid understanding of how to make money on Facebook with affiliate marketing and be well on your way to building a successful and profitable business. So, grab a cup of tea and let's dive in!

Index

1. Join an affiliate network: This is a great starting point as they provide a platform for you to find and promote products.

2. Choose the right products: Research and select products that are in demand and relevant to your target audience.
3. Create a Facebook business page: This will serve as your platform for promoting your affiliate products.
4. Use eye-catching visuals: Make use of images and videos to grab the attention of your audience.
5. Share valuable content: Educate your audience on the benefits of the products you are promoting.
6. Utilize Facebook groups: Join and participate in groups related to your niche, and share your affiliate links in a non-spammy way.
7. Run Facebook ads: Use targeted ads to reach a wider audience and drive more traffic to your affiliate products.
8. Leverage influencer marketing: Collaborate with influencers in your niche to promote your affiliate products to their followers.
9. Host a Facebook Live: Engage with your audience and promote your affiliate products in a live and interactive way.
10. Create a Facebook Shop: This will allow you to sell your affiliate products directly on your Facebook business page.
11. Use retargeting ads: Target people who have already visited your affiliate product pages with tailored ads.
12. Utilize email marketing: Build a list of subscribers and promote your affiliate products through email marketing.
13. Utilize paid social media marketing: Make use of platforms such as Instagram and Pinterest to drive more traffic to your affiliate products.
14. Provide excellent customer service: Ensure that you provide excellent customer support to

maintain a good reputation and retain customers.
15. Continuously optimize your campaigns: Regularly analyze your results and make changes to improve the performance of your affiliate marketing campaigns.
16. By following these 15 ways, you'll be well on your way to making money on Facebook with Affiliate Marketing.

Chapter- 1

Join an affiliate network: This is a great starting point as they provide a platform for you to find and promote products.

-
Joining an affiliate network is an excellent starting point for anyone looking to make money with affiliate marketing on Facebook. An affiliate network is a marketplace where merchants and affiliates (publishers) come together to promote products and services. The merchants offer a commission to affiliates who drive sales through their unique referral links. This is a win-win situation for both parties as the merchants get more sales, and the affiliates earn a commission for each sale made through their links.
-
-
By joining an affiliate network, you have access to a wide range of products to promote. This saves you time and effort in finding products to promote and allows you to focus on promoting the products that are most relevant to your target audience. Most affiliate networks have a variety of categories, from fashion and beauty to technology and home goods,

allowing you to find products that align with your interests and niche.

•

•

In addition to providing a platform to find and promote products, affiliate networks also offer tools and resources to help you succeed. This may include training materials, performance tracking, and reporting, and access to customer support. Some affiliate networks even have a dedicated account manager to help you with your campaigns and offer guidance on how to optimize your performance.

•

•

Another benefit of joining an affiliate network is the ability to participate in affiliate programs offered by multiple merchants. This allows you to promote a variety of products, which can lead to a more diversified income stream. Furthermore, by participating in multiple programs, you have access to a wider range of products, which can help you reach a wider audience.

•

•

In conclusion, joining an affiliate network is a great way to make money on Facebook with affiliate marketing. By joining an affiliate network, you have access to a wide range of products, tools and resources to help you succeed, and the ability to participate in multiple affiliate programs offered by multiple merchants. This provides you with the best opportunity to build a profitable affiliate marketing business on Facebook. So, sign up to an affiliate network today and start making money on Facebook with affiliate marketing!

Chapter- 2

Choose the right products: Research and select products that are in demand and relevant to your target audience.

-
Choosing the right products to promote is essential for success in affiliate marketing on Facebook. By selecting products that are in demand and relevant to your target audience, you increase your chances of making sales and earning a commission. Here's how to choose the right products for your affiliate marketing business on Facebook.

-
-
Research the market: Start by researching the market and identifying products that are in demand and popular with your target audience. Look for products that solve a problem or offer a solution, as these tend to be more successful.

-
-
Consider your niche: Consider your niche and choose products that align with your interests and expertise. This will make it easier for you to create engaging content and promote the products effectively.

-
-
Consider the commission: Choose products that offer a high commission, as this will increase your earning potential. However, don't sacrifice quality for commission, as the goal is to promote products that are in demand and relevant to your target audience.

-
-
Look for a reputable merchant: Make sure to choose a reputable merchant that offers a quality product and has a good reputation in the market. This will help to

build trust with your audience and increase the chances of making a sale.

-
-

Consider the product's page: Look at the product page and make sure that it is professional, well-designed, and provides all the information your audience needs to make a decision.

-
-

By considering these factors, you can choose the right products to promote on Facebook and increase your chances of success in affiliate marketing. Remember, your goal is to promote products that are in demand, relevant to your target audience, and offer a high commission, so take your time and choose wisely!

Chapter- 3

Create a Facebook business page: This will serve as your platform for promoting your affiliate products.

-

Creating a Facebook business page is an important step in making money with affiliate marketing on Facebook. A Facebook business page provides you with a platform to promote your affiliate products and reach a wider audience. Here's how to create a Facebook business page and start promoting your affiliate products.

-
-

Step 1: Set up a Facebook account: If you don't already have a Facebook account, sign up for one. This will serve as the foundation for your Facebook business page.

-

-

Step 2: Create a business page: To create a business page, click on the "Create" button on the top right-hand corner of your Facebook home page and select "Page." From there, you will need to choose the type of page you want to create, such as a business or brand page. Fill in your business information, such as your business name, address, and contact information.

-
-

Step 3: Customize your page: Customize your page by adding a profile picture and cover photo that represents your brand. Make sure that the images are high-quality and professional. You can also add a call-to-action button that encourages visitors to take a specific action, such as visiting your website or making a purchase.

-
-

Step 4: Build your audience: Build your audience by inviting friends, family, and colleagues to like your page. You can also run Facebook ads to reach a wider audience and promote your page.

-
-

Step 5: Post regularly: Post regularly to keep your audience engaged and up-to-date on your latest affiliate products. Share content that is relevant to your target audience and provides value, such as tips, tutorials, and product reviews. Make sure to include your affiliate link in each post to make it easy for your audience to make a purchase.

-
-

Step 6: Interact with your audience: Interact with your audience by responding to comments and messages.

This will help to build a relationship with your audience and increase trust and credibility.

•

•

In conclusion, creating a Facebook business page is an important step in making money with affiliate marketing on Facebook. By following these steps, you can create a professional and engaging platform for promoting your affiliate products and reaching a wider audience. So, get started today and start making money with affiliate marketing on Facebook!

Chapter- 4

Use eye-catching visuals: Make use of images and videos to grab the attention of your audience.

•

Using eye-catching visuals is a crucial aspect of promoting affiliate products on Facebook. By making use of images and videos, you can grab the attention of your audience and increase your chances of making a sale. Here's how to use eye-catching visuals to promote your affiliate products on Facebook.

•

•

Images:

•

•

Use high-quality images that showcase the product and its features. Make sure the images are clear and visually appealing.

•

Use product images that are well-lit and in focus. This will help your audience to see the product in detail and make an informed decision.

•

Use infographics, charts, and diagrams to explain complex concepts and information about the product.

•

Videos:

•

•

Use videos to showcase the product in action and demonstrate how it works. This will help your audience to understand the product better and make an informed decision.

•

Use short, engaging videos that are easy to watch and share. This will increase the chances of your videos being shared and reaching a wider audience.

•

Use video testimonials from satisfied customers to build trust and credibility with your audience.

•

By using eye-catching visuals, you can grab the attention of your audience, provide valuable information about the product, and increase the chances of making a sale. Remember, the goal is to make it easy for your audience to understand the product and make an informed decision. So, make use of high-quality images and videos to promote your affiliate products on Facebook and achieve success with affiliate marketing!

Chapter- 5

Share valuable content: Educate your audience on the benefits of the products you are promoting.

•

Sharing valuable content is a key aspect of promoting affiliate products on Facebook. By educating your audience on the benefits of the products you are promoting, you can build trust and credibility with them and increase your chances of making a sale. Here's how to share valuable content to promote your affiliate products on Facebook.

-
-

Product reviews: Share honest and detailed reviews of the products you are promoting. Discuss the benefits and drawbacks of the product and provide your own experience with it. This will help your audience to make an informed decision and trust your recommendations.

-
-

How-to guides and tutorials: Share how-to guides and tutorials that educate your audience on how to use the product and its features. This will help your audience to understand the product better and make the most of it.

-
-

Industry news and updates: Share news and updates from the industry related to the product. This will help your audience to stay up-to-date on the latest trends and developments in the industry.

-
-

Q&A sessions: Share Q&A sessions where you answer questions from your audience about the product and its benefits. This will help you to engage with your audience and build trust and credibility with them.

-
-

Case studies: Share case studies of real-life customers who have successfully used the product. This will help your audience to see the real-life benefits of the product and make an informed decision.

•

•

By sharing valuable content, you can educate your audience on the benefits of the products you are promoting and build trust and credibility with them. The goal is to provide your audience with the information they need to make an informed decision and feel confident in their purchase. So, share valuable content regularly on your Facebook page and start promoting your affiliate products today.

Chapter- 6

Utilize Facebook groups: Join and participate in groups related to your niche, and share your affiliate links in a non-spammy way.

•

Utilizing Facebook groups is a great way to promote affiliate products on Facebook. By joining and participating in groups related to your niche, you can reach a large and engaged audience and share your affiliate links in a non-spammy way. Here's how to utilize Facebook groups to promote your affiliate products.

•

•

Join relevant groups: Join Facebook groups that are related to your niche and have a large and active membership. Look for groups that are focused on topics related to your affiliate products and have a positive and supportive community.

•

•

Participate in discussions: Participate in discussions and offer helpful advice and insights to other members of the group. This will help you to build trust and credibility with the group and establish yourself as an expert in your niche.

•

•

Share valuable content: Share valuable content related to your niche and the products you are promoting. This can include product reviews, how-to guides, industry news and updates, and more.

•

•

Be respectful: When sharing your affiliate links, make sure to do so in a non-spammy way. Avoid posting links in a way that could be considered spammy or disruptive to the group.

•

•

Monitor your results: Monitor the results of your efforts in Facebook groups and adjust your strategy as needed. Look at the number of clicks on your affiliate links, conversions, and other metrics to see what is working well and what needs improvement.

•

•

By utilizing Facebook groups, you can reach a large and engaged audience and promote your affiliate products in a non-spammy way. The goal is to build trust and credibility with your audience and provide valuable information that will help them make an informed decision. So, join relevant Facebook groups, participate in discussions, and start promoting your affiliate products today.

Chapter- 7

Run Facebook ads: Use targeted ads to reach a wider audience and drive more traffic to your affiliate products.

-
   Running Facebook ads is an effective way to reach a wider audience and drive more traffic to your affiliate products. By using targeted ads, you can reach the right people with the right message at the right time and increase your chances of making a sale. Here's how to run Facebook ads to promote your affiliate products.

-
-
   Define your target audience: Determine who your target audience is and what their interests and habits are. Use Facebook's audience insights tool to learn more about your target audience and create a custom audience based on this information.

-
-
   Choose the right ad format: Choose the right ad format for your needs. There are a variety of ad formats available on Facebook, including image ads, video ads, carousel ads, and more. Choose the format that best fits your goals and the message you want to convey.

-
-
   Set your budget and schedule: Set your budget and schedule for your Facebook ad campaign. Determine how much you want to spend on your campaign and how long you want it to run.

-
-
   Create compelling ad copy: Create compelling ad copy that will grab the attention of your target audience and encourage them to click through to your

affiliate product. Use attention-grabbing headlines, clear and concise messaging, and a strong call-to-action.

-
-

Monitor your results: Monitor the results of your Facebook ad campaign and adjust your strategy as needed. Look at metrics such as impressions, clicks, conversions, and cost per conversion to see what is working well and what needs improvement.

-
-

By running Facebook ads, you can reach a wider audience and drive more traffic to your affiliate products. The goal is to reach the right people with the right message at the right time and increase your chances of making a sale. So, set your budget and schedule, create compelling ad copy, and start promoting your affiliate products today.

Chapter- 8

Leverage influencer marketing: Collaborate with influencers in your niche to promote your affiliate products to their followers.

-

Leveraging influencer marketing is an effective way to promote your affiliate products to a large and engaged audience. By collaborating with influencers in your niche, you can reach their followers and gain exposure for your affiliate products. Here's how to leverage influencer marketing to promote your affiliate products.

-
-

Find the right influencer: Find the right influencer for your brand by researching their audience, the content they produce, and their engagement levels. Look for influencers who are passionate about your niche and have a large and engaged following.

-
-

Reach out to the influencer: Reach out to the influencer and introduce yourself and your affiliate products. Explain why their audience would be interested in your products and why they would be a good fit for the influencer's brand.

-
-

Collaborate on content: Collaborate with the influencer to create high-quality content that promotes your affiliate products. This can include product reviews, unboxing videos, demonstrations, and more.

-
-

Monitor your results: Monitor the results of your influencer marketing campaign and adjust your strategy as needed. Look at metrics such as impressions, clicks, conversions, and cost per conversion to see what is working well and what needs improvement.

-
-

By leveraging influencer marketing, you can reach a large and engaged audience and promote your affiliate products in a way that is both effective and authentic. The goal is to build a strong relationship with the influencer and their followers and provide valuable information that will help them make an informed decision. So, find the right influencer, collaborate on content, and start promoting your affiliate products today.

Chapter- 9

Host a Facebook Live: Engage with your audience and promote your affiliate products in a live and interactive way.

- Hosting a Facebook Live is an effective way to engage with your audience and promote your affiliate products in a live and interactive way. By hosting a Facebook Live, you can build a relationship with your audience and showcase your affiliate products in a way that is both engaging and authentic. Here's how to host a Facebook Live to promote your affiliate products.

-
- Plan your Facebook Live: Plan your Facebook Live and decide on the topics you want to cover and the products you want to promote. Choose a topic that is relevant to your target audience and provides value to them.

-
- Promote your Facebook Live: Promote your Facebook Live in advance and encourage your audience to tune in. Share the date, time, and topic of your Facebook Live and ask your audience to share it with their friends.

-
- Engage with your audience: During your Facebook Live, engage with your audience by answering their questions, responding to comments, and promoting your affiliate products. Make sure to keep the conversation lively and interactive.

-

- Follow up after your Facebook Live: After your Facebook Live, follow up with your audience and continue the conversation. Share the recording of your Facebook Live and ask for feedback from your audience.

-
-

By hosting a Facebook Live, you can engage with your audience and promote your affiliate products in a live and interactive way. The goal is to build a relationship with your audience and provide value to them through your Facebook Live. So, plan your Facebook Live, promote it in advance, engage with your audience, and start promoting your affiliate products today!

Chapter- 10

Create a Facebook Shop: This will allow you to sell your affiliate products directly on your Facebook business page.

-

Creating a Facebook Shop is an effective way to sell your affiliate products directly on your Facebook business page. By having a Facebook Shop, you can reach a wider audience and make it easier for them to purchase your affiliate products. Here's how to create a Facebook Shop to sell your affiliate products.

-
-

Set up a Facebook Business Page: If you haven't already, set up a Facebook Business Page for your brand. This will serve as the foundation for your Facebook Shop.

-

-

Set up a Shop: To set up a Shop, go to your Facebook Business Page and click on the "Shop" section. Follow the steps to set up your Shop and add your affiliate products.

-
-

Add your affiliate products: Add your affiliate products to your Facebook Shop, including product images, descriptions, and prices. Make sure to provide as much information as possible to help your audience make an informed decision.

-
-

Promote your Facebook Shop: Promote your Facebook Shop by sharing your products on your Facebook Business Page and with your audience. Encourage your audience to visit your Facebook Shop and purchase your affiliate products.

-
-

Monitor your results: Monitor your results and adjust your strategy as needed. Look at metrics such as impressions, clicks, sales, and cost per sale to see what is working well and what needs improvement.

-
-

By creating a Facebook Shop, you can reach a wider audience and sell your affiliate products directly on your Facebook Business Page. The goal is to make it easy for your audience to purchase your affiliate products and provide a convenient and seamless shopping experience. So, set up your Facebook Shop, add your affiliate products, promote your Shop, and start selling today!

Chapter- 11

Use retargeting ads: Target people who have already visited your affiliate product pages with tailored ads.

-

Using retargeting ads is an effective way to target people who have already visited your affiliate product pages with tailored ads. Retargeting ads allow you to show ads to people who have already shown interest in your affiliate products, increasing the chances of them making a purchase. Here's how to use retargeting ads to promote your affiliate products.

-
-

Set up a retargeting campaign: Set up a retargeting campaign on a platform such as Facebook Ads Manager. Choose the audience you want to target, such as people who have visited your affiliate product pages.

-
-

Create tailored ads: Create tailored ads that are specific to the interests of your target audience. For example, if someone has visited your affiliate product page for a particular product, show them an ad for that product.

-
-

Set your budget: Set your budget for your retargeting campaign. Consider factors such as your target audience size, the cost per click, and the cost per conversion.

-
-

Monitor your results: Monitor your results and adjust your strategy as needed. Look at metrics such as impressions, clicks, conversions, and cost per conversion to see what is working well and what needs improvement.

-
-

By using retargeting ads, you can target people who have already shown interest in your affiliate products, increasing the chances of them making a purchase. The goal is to provide a personalized and relevant shopping experience for your target audience. So, set up your retargeting campaign, create tailored ads, set your budget, and start promoting your affiliate products today!

Chapter- 12

Utilize email marketing: Build a list of subscribers and promote your affiliate products through email marketing.

-

Utilizing email marketing is an effective way to promote your affiliate products to a targeted audience. By building a list of subscribers, you can reach people who have expressed interest in your products and provide them with valuable information and promotions. Here's how to use email marketing to promote your affiliate products.

-
-

Build your email list: Build your email list by offering something of value, such as a free eBook or a discount code, in exchange for a person's email address. You can build your email list through sign-ups on your website or through Facebook Lead Ads.

-
-

Segment your list: Segment your email list based on factors such as subscriber interests, purchase history, and behavior. This will allow you to send targeted and relevant emails to your subscribers.

-
-

Create valuable content: Create valuable content, such as articles, tutorials, and product reviews, that your subscribers will find useful and informative. This will build trust and increase engagement with your subscribers.

-
-

Promote your affiliate products: Promote your affiliate products to your email list by including links in your emails. Make sure to provide clear and concise information about the benefits of the products you are promoting.

-
-

Monitor your results: Monitor your results and adjust your strategy as needed. Look at metrics such as open rates, click-through rates, and conversion rates to see what is working well and what needs improvement.

-
-

By using email marketing, you can reach a targeted audience and promote your affiliate products through valuable and relevant emails. The goal is to build a relationship with your subscribers and provide them with a personalized shopping experience. So, build your email list, segment your list, create valuable content, promote your affiliate products, and start selling today!

Chapter- 13

Utilize paid social media marketing: Make use of platforms such as

Instagram and Pinterest to drive more traffic to your affiliate products.

- Paid social media marketing can be a highly effective way to promote your affiliate products to a wider audience. Platforms such as Instagram and Pinterest offer unique opportunities to reach potential customers and drive more traffic to your affiliate products. Here's how to use paid social media marketing to your advantage:

-
- Determine your target audience: Determine who your target audience is and where they are spending their time on social media. For example, if you are promoting beauty products, your target audience may be found on Instagram.

-
- Create a strategy: Develop a strategy that aligns with your goals and budget. Decide what types of ads you want to run and how often you want to run them.

-
- Create visually appealing ads: Use eye-catching images and videos to grab the attention of your audience. Make sure to include a clear call to action and a link to your affiliate products.

-
- Target your ads: Use the targeting options offered by each platform to reach the right people. This can include targeting by location, interests, behaviors, and more.

-
- Monitor your results: Regularly monitor your results to see what is working well and what needs

improvement. Use metrics such as impressions, clicks, and conversions to determine your success.

-

-

Optimize your ads: Optimize your ads based on your results. Make changes to your targeting, ad format, and messaging as needed to improve your results.

-

-

By utilizing paid social media marketing, you can reach a wider audience and drive more traffic to your affiliate products. Make use of the unique features offered by each platform to create visually appealing ads and target the right people. So, determine your target audience, create a strategy, create visually appealing ads, target your ads, monitor your results, and optimize your ads for maximum success!

Chapter- 14

Provide excellent customer service: Ensure that you provide excellent customer support to maintain a good reputation and retain customers.

-

Providing excellent customer service is a crucial aspect of any successful affiliate marketing business. By ensuring that you provide top-notch support to your customers, you can build a good reputation, retain customers, and increase your chances of success. Here's how to provide excellent customer service in your affiliate marketing business:

-

-

Respond promptly: Respond promptly to customer inquiries and complaints. This will show that you value your customers and are committed to providing them with the best possible experience.

-
-

Be helpful: Be helpful and informative when responding to customer inquiries. Provide clear and concise answers that address the customer's concerns or needs.

-
-

Listen actively: Listen actively to your customers to understand their needs and concerns. Ask questions to clarify any issues and ensure that you are providing the right information and support.

-
-

Empathize with customers: Empathize with your customers and put yourself in their shoes. Show that you understand their perspective and are committed to finding a solution that meets their needs.

-
-

Follow up: Follow up with customers to ensure that their needs have been met and that they are satisfied with your services.

-
-

Continuously improve: Continuously monitor and evaluate your customer service processes to identify areas for improvement. Make changes to your processes as needed to provide even better customer support.

-
-

By providing excellent customer service, you can build a good reputation, retain customers, and increase your chances of success in the long run. Respond promptly, be helpful, listen actively, empathize with customers, follow up, and continuously improve your customer service processes for the best results.

Chapter- 15

Continuously optimize your campaigns: Regularly analyze your results and make changes to improve the performance of your affiliate marketing campaigns.

-
  Continuous optimization of your affiliate marketing campaigns is crucial for achieving success. By regularly analyzing your results and making changes to improve your campaigns, you can ensure that your efforts are paying off and that you are achieving your desired results. Here's how to continuously optimize your affiliate marketing campaigns:
-
-
  Regularly review your results: Regularly review your results to see how your campaigns are performing. Use metrics such as conversion rates, click-through rates, and revenue to assess the success of your campaigns.
-
-
  Identify areas for improvement: Identify areas for improvement by analyzing your results and looking for trends and patterns. Pay attention to the metrics that matter most to your business and focus on improving those areas.
-
-
  Make changes: Based on your analysis, make changes to your campaigns to improve their performance. This may involve adjusting your

targeting, adjusting your creative elements, or experimenting with new strategies.
-
-

Test and refine: Test your changes and refine your campaigns based on the results. Continuously test and refine your campaigns to ensure that you are getting the best results possible.
-
-

Stay up-to-date: Stay up-to-date on the latest trends and best practices in affiliate marketing. This will help you to stay ahead of the curve and continuously optimize your campaigns for the best results.
-
-

Continuously optimizing your affiliate marketing campaigns is a key factor in achieving success. Regularly review your results, identify areas for improvement, make changes, test and refine your campaigns, and stay up-to-date on the latest trends and best practices to achieve your desired results.